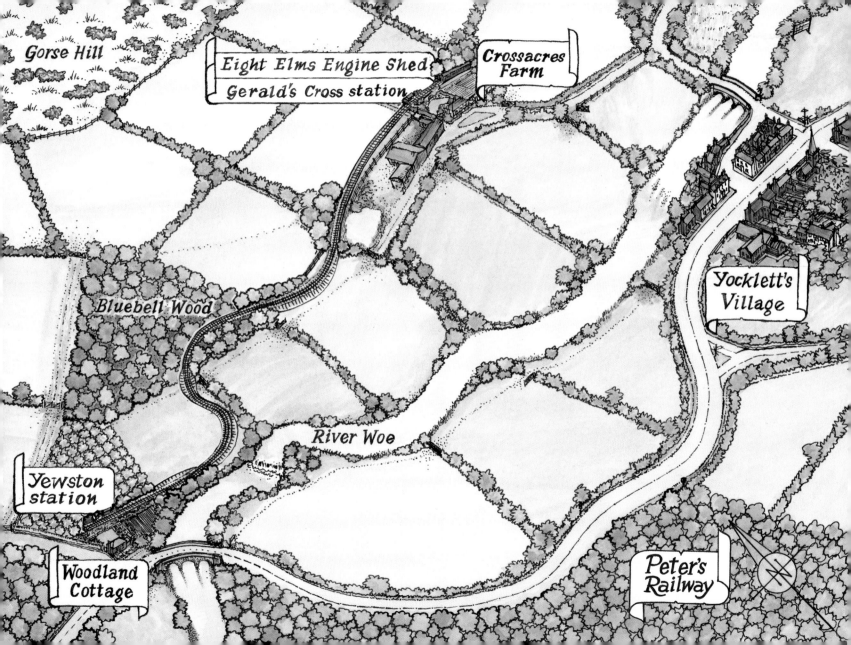

Gorse Hill

Eight Elms Engine Shed
Gerald's Cross station

Crossacres Farm

Bluebell Wood

Yocklett's Village

River Woe

Yewston station

Woodland Cottage

Peter's Railway

Peter's Railway
and the
Moonlight Express

Published by Christopher Vine 2009

All rights reserved. No part of this publication may be
reproduced, stored in a retrieval system, or transmitted in
any form by any means, electronic, mechanical,
photocopied, or otherwise, or recorded by any other
information storage and retrieval system, without prior
permission in writing from the author.
Christopher Vine asserts his moral rights.

Printed by The Amadeus Press
Cleckheaton, West Yorkshire,
England.

All rights reserved
Copyright © 2009 Christopher Vine

ISBN 978-0-9553359-2-1

Foreword

I believe, and many to whom I have spoken agree, that some of us are born with a love of railways but it may lie latent until aroused by experience or by books like this.

It was my dream to have my own railway. Now I have my own standard-gauge railway, complete with steam engines, in my garden..... which proves that dreams can come true!

Not everyone can have their own railway on which to visit Grandpa but dreams and planning cost nothing and are very pleasurable. As you will see in this book; you can also travel on the Romney Hythe & Dymchurch Railway which I have the honour to Chair. It is a main-line railway one-quarter full-size but with all the excitement and problems of the big railway.

Having spent my whole life constructing things, including full-size railways, huge buildings, power stations, oil drilling platforms, The Dome ! .. it is great to find a book which will inspire children to want to make things.

Not only will this book inspire them, it also provides plenty of clear information on how things work and how they are made. We need engineers now more than ever and I believe this book will encourage embryo engineers to believe they can realize their dreams.

Thank you Chris Vine for two such lovely books. Please can we have the next volume soon.

The Hon Sir William McAlpine Bt. F.I.L.T., F.R.S.E.,

The watercolour illustrations are by John Wardle.

Living on a Farm with a Railway

Peter lives in Woodland Cottage at the edge of a farm, with his Mum and Dad, Jo and Colin. Peter has a little brother and sister, the twins Harry and Kitty. They are still very small and take up a lot of Mum's time because they can't do much for themselves.

Peter's Grandpa Gerald lives at Crossacres Farm with Grandma Pat. Sharing the house with them is a sporty Jack Russell dog called Minnie and the slinky and very dotty cat, Cato. It's a lovely place to live with fields and woods all around them. Just down the road is the village of Yockletts where Peter goes to school.

Crossacres Farm is a very busy place and there is always something going on. Every day the cows need milking and moving between fields. Sometimes the sheep escape through holes in a fence and have to be chased back into their field and then there are tractors to drive and fields of corn which need looking after.

Last summer Peter and Grandpa built a miniature steam railway between their two houses, across the farmland. They built it because they get on so well together that they like to be able to visit each other whenever they want and it's too far to walk along the twisty road. The route between their two houses by road is over two miles but, across the fields, only a little over half a mile.

Their railway takes a very pretty and scenic route past the duck pond, across several fields, through Bluebell Wood and beside the River Woe. Most people would just use a car but Grandpa doesn't own one and anyway, the journey by train is much more fun.

It was a lot of hard work to make, but they are very pleased they took all the trouble to build the railway. It has given them and their friends and family so much pleasure. They have clocked up hundreds of miles so far and use the train whenever they need it, or just for fun if it is a nice day or they have friends visiting.

It takes a long time to light the fire in the engine and get up steam and there are lots of things to do, but this makes it more interesting. Peter oils the engine, fills the tender and boiler with water and lights the fire. Grandpa has always done the driving until now.

Sometimes Grandpa gets up steam to visit Peter and his family in Woodland Cottage. At other times Peter wants to go and visit his grandparents at Crossacres Farm, so he telephones Grandpa and asks him to bring the train over to pick him up.

Of course, once the locomotive has the fire lit and steam is up, they

usually do several runs just because it is such a good way of spending an afternoon. And as a bonus, no one can find them to ask them to do any boring chores. They can enjoy the scenery as they pass through the farm and Grandpa can check that all his animals and crops are in good order.

Apart from being very busy on the farm, Grandpa likes to spend as much time as he can in his workshop. It looks a bit like a shed from the outside, but inside there are lots of special tools and machines which Grandpa uses to make things. Last year he and Peter made all of the track and carriages for the railway in the workshop. He usually has one or two projects under construction. Sometimes

it is something useful for Grandma like her new wheelbarrow, or perhaps it is a splendid toy for Peter such as the go-kart he made a few years ago.

At the moment he is making some modifications to his old lawn mower as he wants to try an experiment. He has decided that if he could tie one end of a strong piece of string to the mower and the other end to a peg in the middle of the lawn, it might cut the

grass by itself. His idea is that as it goes round and round, the string will get wrapped onto the peg, pulling the mower inwards until all the grass has been cut. Grandpa can then get on with something more interesting in the workshop instead of spending hours mowing the grass.

When they built the railway last summer they had been very lucky to meet Mr Esmond. He had saved them a lot of time and work by lending them his wonderful steam locomotive Fiery Fox. It would have taken them many years to make the engine themselves and to buy one would have been much too expensive. So they were very grateful to Mr Esmond and he has become a good friend. They sometimes ask him to come over to play trains and have lunch with them.

Mr Esmond lives in a house with a small garden where there isn't room to build a railway so he is very happy that his engine has a track to run on. He is always pleased to visit the farm because it gives him the chance to drive his locomotive on a really good railway. Sometimes he just likes to sit on an old tree stump beside the line and watch his engine steam past, pulling the train. It always gives him a lot of pleasure to see something he has made with his own hands, working so well. There are no nasty clanking or squeaking noises and it always runs very smoothly and powerfully. The only sounds are the ringing of the wheels on the rails with the clickety click as they pass over the joints. And of course the chuffing as the exhaust steam blasts up the chimney.

Before he went home one evening, Mr Esmond was talking to Peter and Grandpa. "I have seen how careful you are with Fiery Fox," he said to Peter. "I think you should have a go at driving her."

"Keep it simple at first," he continued. "Just concentrate on the main controls: The regulator to control the steam, like the accelerator pedal in a car. The reverser to make her go forwards or backwards, a bit like a car gearbox. And most importantly, the brakes. If you get into any difficulty, Grandpa will be there to help you out."

"Thank you," Peter grinned. "I'll be very careful, don't you worry!"

"Just don't forget to watch the water level in the boiler," warned Mr Esmond, smiling. "We don't want to have an explosion you know!"

Peter wanted to know what happened when a boiler exploded.

"When a steam boiler explodes," explained Mr Esmond, "all the high pressure steam escapes at once. And most of the boiling water in the boiler turns to steam at the same time. It all goes off with a great roaring bang and bits of the boiler are thrown a long way away."

"There was one engine, No. 510," he continued, "which blew up with such force that the whole of the outside of the boiler disappeared completely. Some bits of it were found 200 metres away. All of the inside fire tubes could suddenly be seen because the casing had gone. The steam had escaped with so much force that all the tubes were bent and broken. Some were even wrapped round the smokebox and chimney!"

Peter looked a bit worried by all this but Mr Esmond explained that it happened a long time ago in 1877 and that nobody was hurt as the driver and fireman had luckily been filling the tender at the time of the explosion.

Peter then remembered about learning to drive Fiery Fox. "Can we have a steam-up tomorrow Grandpa?" he asked excitedly. "I can't wait to try driving."

"Not tomorrow Peter," said Grandpa smiling. "Tomorrow I have got something different planned for you and me."

"It's your birthday soon and as your present from me, I thought I would take you on an expedition to the Romney Hythe and Dymchurch Railway."

Peter had heard of the railway but immediately wanted to know more about it.

"It is one of the best miniature railways in the country if not in the whole world," said Grandpa. "Captain J.E.P. Howey built it in 1925 simply because he wanted to build a railway. He was a very rich and famous racing driver and he planned to build it with his great friend Count Louis Zborowski, another famous racing driver."

Unfortunately the Count was killed in a motor race and so he did not see his wonderful railway finished. He had however, already ordered the first two locomotives for the railway: Green Goddess and Northern Chief.

"Driving cars fast is very dangerous," said Grandpa to Peter seriously "and he was killed when his car flew off the road and hit a tree. It was left to Captain Howey and the great engineer Henry Greenly to plan and build it."

"What sort of railway did they build?" asked Peter.

Grandpa explained that it was a quarter of the full-size, or about twice as big as their own. It was such a success that it made the whole area along the coast popular as a holiday destination. The local children even used it to get to school instead of a bus and they still do.

It originally connected the towns and villages of New Romney, Hythe and Dymchurch. A few years later they built an extension out onto the stony wasteland called Dungeness.

"We can go tomorrow," said Grandpa, who was looking forward to it himself. "I hope you enjoy it."

"It sounds amazing," Peter said. "I don't know how I will get to sleep tonight, thinking about it!"

The Boiler - How the Locomotive Makes Its Steam

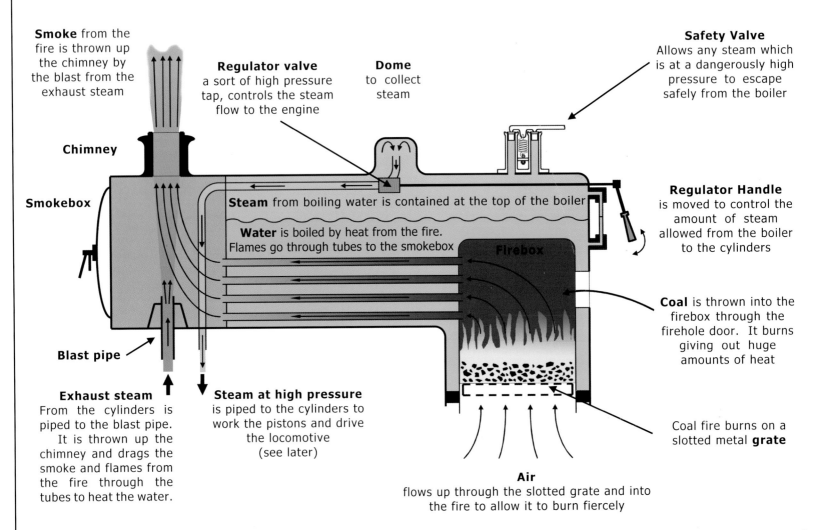

Smoke from the fire is thrown up the chimney by the blast from the exhaust steam

Regulator valve a sort of high pressure tap, controls the steam flow to the engine

Dome to collect steam

Safety Valve Allows any steam which is at a dangerously high pressure to escape safely from the boiler

Chimney

Smokebox

Steam from boiling water is contained at the top of the boiler

Water is boiled by heat from the fire. Flames go through tubes to the smokebox

Firebox

Regulator Handle is moved to control the amount of steam allowed from the boiler to the cylinders

Coal is thrown into the firebox through the firehole door. It burns giving out huge amounts of heat

Blast pipe

Exhaust steam From the cylinders is piped to the blast pipe. It is thrown up the chimney and drags the smoke and flames from the fire through the tubes to heat the water.

Steam at high pressure is piped to the cylinders to work the pistons and drive the locomotive (see later)

Coal fire burns on a slotted metal **grate**

Air flows up through the slotted grate and into the fire to allow it to burn fiercely

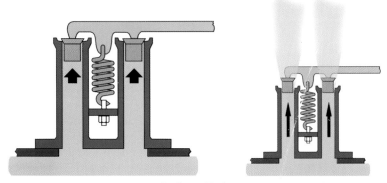

Safety Valve

The safety valve releases steam from the boiler if the pressure reaches a dangerous level. Normally the plungers (pink) are held down by the spring and lever and keep the steam inside the boiler.

When the pressure gets too high, the steam pushes the plungers up, stretching the spring, and the steam can escape safely.

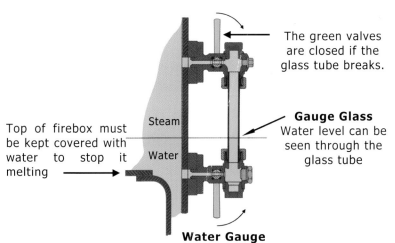

The green valves are closed if the glass tube breaks.

Steam

Gauge Glass
Water level can be seen through the glass tube

Top of firebox must be kept covered with water to stop it melting

Water

Water Gauge

The water gauge has a glass tube so that the driver can see the level of the water in the boiler. It is very important that the water level is kept above the top of the metal firebox to stop it from melting and causing an explosion.

Boiler EXPLOSION!

This is what can happen if the safety valve fails to operate or if there is a fault in the boiler shell. In this photograph, taken in about 1850, almost the whole of the outside of the boiler has disappeared and landed in a field 50 metres away. A small part of it has landed at the bottom left of the picture.

All of the tubes which carry the fire and heat from the firebox to the smokebox and chimney are now clearly visible. The force of the explosion has bent the tubes outwards.

After all the heat from the fire has been absorbed by the hot water and steam, there is a huge amount of energy contained in a boiler. If there is a failure it is a bit like a powerful bomb.

This is a very old fashioned type of locomotive but the destructive power of steam has never changed.

The Romney Hythe and Dymchurch Railway

The next day, Peter's Dad drove them to the railway station so they could catch a train for their day out. On the way Grandpa told Peter a bit about the railway they were going to see.

Once they were settled in the train, Grandpa asked Peter "Did I ever tell you about the time when I went with two friends driving a locomotive between New Romney and Hythe?"

"No, but it sounds very exciting," replied Peter. "However did you wangle that, Grandpa?"

"Well," he explained, "they have some special training days when you can pay to be taught to drive one of their locomotives. Two friends and I took it in turns to drive. There is room in the cab for two people, one of us and the regular driver, Dave, who was showing us what to do."

"We steamed up and down the line all day with one of us driving and the other two riding in one of the carriages behind the engine." Grandpa was smiling as he remembered how much fun it had been.

"Wow!" said Peter. "That sounds like the most fantastic day out ever."

"It was," agreed Grandpa. "It was quite expensive but if you measure excitement, thrills and pleasure against the cost, I think it was probably the best value for money I have ever spent."

"It also made me realize how difficult it is to be a good engine driver. You have to start the train without jolting and, at each station, you have to stop smoothly at exactly the right place. The stopping part is really much more difficult than the driving. And all the time you have to keep a watchful eye on the signals to make sure you stop if there is any danger."

"The locomotive we drove was called Green Goddess," he remembered. "I wonder if we will be lucky and have her and Dave hauling our train today? I hope it is, because he will probably let you look in the cab."

The nearest railway station to Hythe was a few miles away so they had to catch a bus. Compared to the train, the bus was very bouncy and noisy but at least it got them to where they wanted.

When they got to Hythe station, Grandpa bought the tickets for a round trip to Dungeness and back again. It would be a 27 mile journey by miniature steam train. They would get off at New Romney where they could have lunch and visit the railway's museum. Then, if there was time, they would ask if they could have a look in the engine shed.

There was nearly an hour before their train was due to leave so they had plenty of time to look around the station. Walking to the end of the platform they found the signal box from where the signalman controlled all the signals and points for the station. Just beside the signal box was a large turntable.

"You know how on our railway," began Grandpa, "when we get to the end of the line, we have to run the engine backwards on the return trip? Well here they have a turntable where they can turn the engine around so it's facing the right way."

Grandpa, being a bit cheeky, asked the signalman if they could look inside.

"Of course," said the signalman. "Come in! It's a really good place to watch the trains from as you can see everything from here and I can tell you what's going on."

They had only just got into the signal box when a bell rang and the signalman pressed a bell button to reply. "That means the train is just coming into my section of track," he said. "It will be arriving here in just a minute or two."

Peter thought it was fun being at the very heart of the whole operation.

They watched out of the window, looking up the line. They could see the signals on a gantry over the tracks with their semaphore arms and red and green lamps. Trains must stop when the signal arm is level and the light shows red. However the signal over the track entering the station was down with a green light ready to allow a train to come in.

In the distance they could hear the unmistakable sound of a steam whistle announcing the arrival of the train. They watched and waited. Then around the corner it came, quite slowly with a beautiful green locomotive at the front. It was Green Goddess with driver Dave at the controls. It whistled again as it passed the signal box and then glided almost silently into the platform, stopping a little way before the buffers at the end of the line.

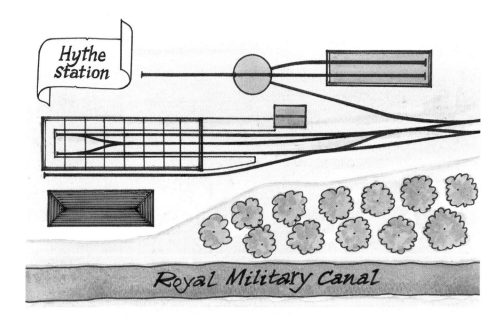

Peter had never seen such a lovely sight. Everything was so perfect. The track curving away into the distance, the sun glinting off the engine and the wonderful movement of all the parts of the locomotive. It was like poetry in motion.

"Oh Grandpa," whispered Peter. "Did you really get to drive that engine?"

Peter and Grandpa watched from the signal box as the driver turned the engine. First he uncoupled it from the train and drove it forwards over some points. Then he drove backwards up a track beside the carriages and then onto the turntable.

When the driver had put the brakes on, the signalman went out and very slowly pushed the turntable round by hand. Next, the locomotive drove off the turntable, over some points and back onto the main line. Then it was just a simple matter to reverse the engine down onto the train and couple up ready for the next run.

As Green Goddess reversed past the signal box, Grandpa waved to Dave the driver and Dave, who recognized him straight away, tooted the whistle as a greeting.

All the time, the signalman was controlling the points by pulling levers in the signal box. The levers pulled rods outside which moved the points to switch the locomotive or trains from one track to another.

They thanked the signalman for inviting them in and walked over to the platform so they could have a good look at the locomotive.

"Wouldn't it be great," Peter said as they walked, "to have a turntable at both ends of our railway. Then we could always drive the train with the engine facing forwards. It would be much easier and we could go a lot faster."

Grandpa agreed, but said that it would be an awful lot of work to build two turntables.

"Never mind for the moment," he said. "Let's go and have a look at the engine."

Green Goddess was long and sleek and painted a lovely shade of green, just like Fiery Fox. Grandpa told Peter that she was a miniature version of the LNER locomotive, Flying Scotsman and that she was built way back in 1925. That was before even Grandpa was born.

When the locomotives were new, one of them was taken by lorry and displayed next to a full size one to show the difference in size.

They looked at Green Goddess for a few minutes and chatted with Dave. Then it was time to jump on for the first part of their trip.

There were several different sorts of carriages making up the train and, as it was a fine day, Peter and Grandpa chose one with no doors and windows quite near

the front. It would be fun to be able to hear the engine working and to smell the mixture of smoke, hot oil and steam coming from her chimney.

The journey started with the line running alongside an old canal. On the other side of the railway were houses, with their gardens coming right down to the side of the track.

After a while they left the town behind and were out in the flat country of the Romney Marsh. Here Green Goddess really got into her stride and the train went along at a terrific pace, rocking gently from side to side. The chuffs from her exhaust steam blurred into a purring noise as she got on with the job of hauling the heavy train.

There were a couple of stops on the way to New Romney for small village stations. Peter noticed that some of the houses next to the line had little dens at the bottom of their gardens for children to watch the trains go by.

"I think we will have a very quick lunch first," said Grandpa. "Once we get into the museum and engine shed we will want to be there for so long we will forget all about eating. Then we'll be hungry for the rest of the day."

Lunch finished, they went upstairs to the museum and model railway exhibition. There were lots of old photographs of the railway taken while it was being built. Captain Howey certainly seemed to have a lot of men to help him build it. There was also the most wonderful model railway that Peter had ever seen. It looped round the room and even climbed mountains so that it could go over the top of a door. It was very realistic and there were always several trains moving at once.

Peter could have stayed watching it for hours but Grandpa said that if he wanted to look in the engine shed, they had better get moving.

They walked down the path to the shed and found one of the drivers who agreed to show them around. The shed had three tracks or roads with engines stabled nose to tail. There were two or three engines on each road, all covered with blankets to protect them. Sleeping beauties.

Soon it was time to catch the train onwards to Dungeness. This time it was a different locomotive, 'Hercules'. She was a deep maroon red colour and had been designed to haul really heavy trains. Grandpa showed Peter that Hercules had eight driving wheels compared to the six on Green Goddess. They were slightly smaller in diameter too, which would mean they would have to turn faster to go at the same speed.

Then the guard blew his whistle and they had to jump onto the train quickly or they would have been left behind.

Steam Locomotive Wheel Arrangements - The Code

There are two types of wheels on locomotives. The main driving wheels which push the engine forward and do all the work are shown red in the diagrams below. There can also be smaller carrying wheels which carry some of the engine's weight and spread the load out along the track.

The number of wheels a locomotive has and the way they are arranged is usually described with a simple code, for example 4-2-2. The first digit is the number of carrying wheels in front of the driving wheels, the second digit is the number of driving wheels and the last digit is the number of carrying wheels behind the drivers. On the first engine below, there are 4 carrying wheels ahead of the 2 drivers and 2 carrying wheels behind making it a 4-2-2. (Don't forget that the diagrams only show one side of the engine or half the number of wheels.) The code does not count any wheels under a tender for carrying coal and water behind the engine.

Carrying wheels are useful on a fast or express engine because they can guide it along the track, especially on curves, making it nice and steady at high speeds. However the carrying wheels take some of the weight of the engine away from the driving wheels which means that the engine may slip more easily. So for a goods engine which is designed to pull very heavy loads slowly, it is usually better to have fewer or no carrying wheels so that the drivers take all the weight and can get a good grip on the rails.

An example of an express type of engine is the 4-6-2 (like Green Goddess or Flying Scotsman) where only 6 out of the 12 wheels are driving. However a typical heavy goods locomotive would be an 0-8-0 where all of the weight is on the driving wheels.

Some wheel arrangements are so common they have been given names such as 'Pacific' or 'Atlantic'.

(Just to confuse, when saying any zeros in the code, they are usually pronounces as "o" (oh). So the code is "oh-8-oh" instead of "nought-8-nought" or "zero-8-zero".)

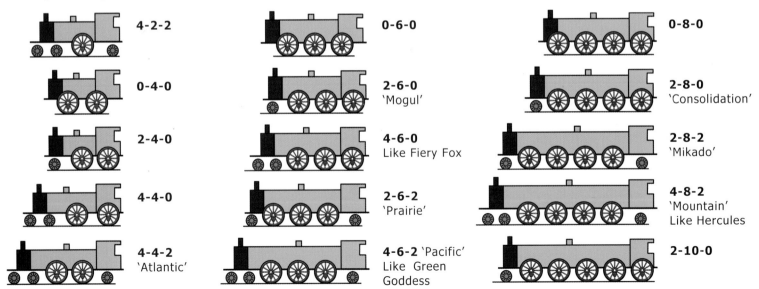

4-2-2	0-6-0	0-8-0
0-4-0	2-6-0 'Mogul'	2-8-0 'Consolidation'
2-4-0	4-6-0 Like Fiery Fox	2-8-2 'Mikado'
4-4-0	2-6-2 'Prairie'	4-8-2 'Mountain' Like Hercules
4-4-2 'Atlantic'	4-6-2 'Pacific' Like Green Goddess	2-10-0

Can You Crack the Code?

See if you can work out the code for the wheel arrangements for these locomotives.

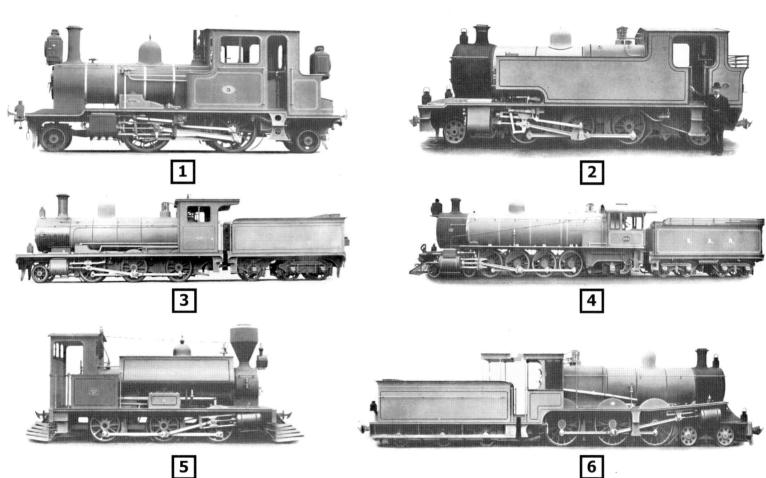

1

2

3

4

5

6

1. 2-4-2   2. 2-6-2   3. 2-6-0
4. 4-8-2   5. 0-6-0   6. 4-6-0

Onwards to Dungeness

The journey into the wilderness of Dungeness took quite a long time over the enormous shingle beach, but eventually they arrived at the station. It was in the middle of nowhere but strangely beautiful. There was almost nothing in sight except two lighthouses and two gigantic nuclear power stations. A few wooden houses were dotted about, some of them made from the bodies of old railway carriages, just sitting on the pebbles.

There was plenty of time before the next train so Peter and Grandpa bought tickets to go up the old lighthouse. Peter counted 169 steps as they wound their way up the spiral staircase. Once there, the view was spectacular and they could see for miles.

Peter had not noticed before, but the railway here was only single track instead of the double track for the rest of the railway. Not many trains used the Dungeness section so it was cheaper to have just one line with trains for both directions sharing it. To avoid any risk of head on collisions there was a strict rule which only allowed one train at a time onto the single track section.

The railway looked like a toy from their vantage point and there was one thing of great interest to Peter. Looking down at the track he could see it went round in a large loop and joined back on itself. This meant the trains could run round the loop and be facing back towards New Romney for the return journey. This 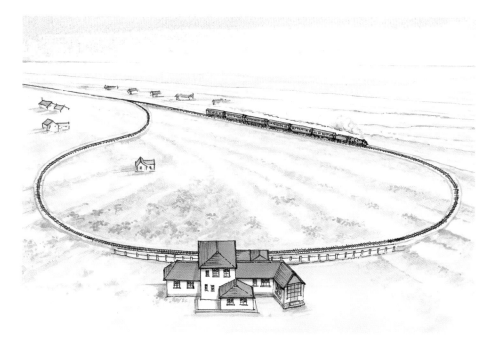 had saved the railway a lot of expense and effort because they had not had to build another turntable to turn the engines. The only thing they had needed was the space to build the loop, a bit of track and a set of points where the loop joined back onto the main line.

At Dungeness there was plenty of space for the loop, but in the town at Hythe there was only room for a turntable.

Peter was thoughtful. "Grandpa," he said after a while. "Do you think we could build a turntable at your end of our railway, just beside Eight Elms Shed, then perhaps we could build a turning loop at my end of the railway at Woodland Cottage?"

"Yes," agreed Grandpa. "That's a really good idea. There's plenty of space behind your house for a loop and it would save us the work of making a second turntable."

"There's another advantage too. It would give us a really long run because we would be able to steam from the farm, all the way to Woodland Cottage and back again without stopping. We will just go round the loop and head back."

Peter thought this was a great scheme and said "If it was good enough for Captain Howey, it's good enough for me!"

"Building a turntable and loop sounds like a good project for us, Peter," said Grandpa. "And it should keep you out of mischief for the summer holiday," he chuckled.

It was getting quite late, so the two of them went back down the spiral stairs and out to the station to await the arrival of their train to take them back to Hythe.

It wasn't long before they saw the smoke and steam in the distance and they enjoyed watching the train get closer and closer. As it pulled into the station, they were really pleased to see that Green Goddess and Dave were in charge.

"I've been all the way to Hythe and back since I last saw you two," he laughed when they came up to talk to him. "And I'm glad to see you again Peter because I've got an idea…."

"The thing is," he went on, "there aren't many people around at this time of day and you're not too big. If you kept you head down, I don't think anyone would notice if you rode with me in the cab for the journey back to Hythe. I can't let you drive, but you could see everything I do and you could enjoy the view through the cab window. You can see forward up the track as we steam along. Would you like that?"

Peter was so excited he could hardly speak. "Are you serious?" he spluttered. "I would love to!" And before Dave could change his mind, Peter jumped into the cab and sat down, getting himself out of sight.

"I'll see you again at Hythe," smiled Grandpa as he went to get into the front carriage of the train.

Riding Home in the Cab

The first thing Peter noticed when he got into the cab of Green Goddess was the heat from the back of the boiler. Although it was evening and the air had turned chilly, it was warm as toast in the cab.

Before they set off, Dave wanted to make sure the fire was really hot and that there was plenty of coal in it. He opened the firehole door and the cab got even hotter. Peter looked into the firebox and could see the flames and the red hot bed of the coal fire. With the engine stopped, the fire was burning quite gently and he could see the flames lazily licking into the tubes which went through the boiler. The tubes took the flames and hot gases through the water to the smokebox and chimney at the front, heating the water on their way.

"That's alright Peter," said Dave. "There's enough fire in there to get us going for a few miles and then we can put some coal on while we're running."

Just then the guard blew his whistle and it was time to go.

Dave wound the engine's reverser from neutral or 'mid gear' into full forward gear, released the brake and very gently opened the steam regulator. Green Goddess moved forward very slowly at first as she started to pull the heavy train.

There was a great whooshing of steam from some pipes low down at the front.

"What's all that steam?" asked Peter, a little alarmed.

Dave explained that when the locomotive stood still for a while, the cylinders would cool off a little. "The trouble is that when we start again, the cold cylinders will cool the steam so that some of it turns back into water. This could damage the engine so there are drain valves which I can open for the first few metres when we start. Any water and some steam gets blown out through the drains and that's what you can see."

Then he pulled a lever to shut the drains and the clouds of steam at the front of the locomotive disappeared. Now Peter could hear the engine beginning to work with the usual loud chuffs of exhaust steam going up the chimney.

Little by little the locomotive built up speed until they were running at the speed limit for the line. The exhaust noise had become a sort of purring roar. The wheels were ringing on the rails and there was a tremendous heat from the firebox. Green Goddess hurtled along the track, rolling and heaving, for all the world like a wild animal, only just in the control of her driver.

It was starting to get dark now and Peter was thrilled and terrified all at the same time. Then Dave opened the firehole door to put some more coal on.

The fire, which earlier had been red hot and lazy, was now a furious white hot storm. The engine was working hard and the exhaust steam in the chimney was drawing the fire through the tubes of the boiler to make more steam to replace the steam which was being used. It was like looking into the heart of a volcano.

Peter looked at Dave, his face lit up brightly by the fire. He was concentrating hard but looking quite content and Peter realized that this was all perfectly normal, so he settled down to enjoy the ride.

After a while, Dave operated some valves in the cab to put some water into the boiler to keep it at a safe level. Peter looked at the glass water gauge and could see the level starting to rise.

Mile after mile they plunged along the now dark railway. Regularly Dave put more coal on the fire and topped up the water. There were a few stops at stations but all too soon they were pulling into Hythe station at the end of the line.

Grandpa appeared beside the engine and he and Peter thanked Driver Dave for a wonderful adventure and promised to visit again soon. Peter didn't really know the right words to tell Dave how much he had enjoyed the trip, but he did his best.

On the way home, Peter and Grandpa discussed how they were going to make the turntable and turning loop on their own railway and also made one really good decision: They would dcfinitcly run trains in the dark!

Points, Switches or Turnouts

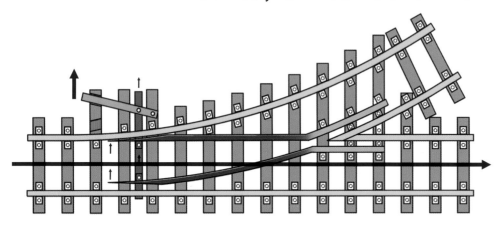

Points are used to switch trains from one track to another.

They have special rails called 'blades' or 'switch' rails (red) which can be moved from side to side. The ordinary rails are shown in yellow.

The green lever is moved to set the points. Set one way and the train goes straight through. Moved the other way and the train is turned off the straight track and onto the curved part to go onto a siding or maybe a branch line.

On a full size railway the operating lever would usually be further away and connected to the points by long rods.

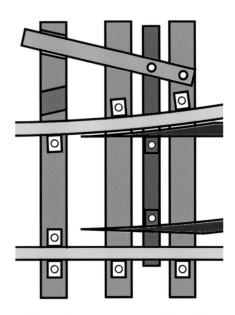

The lever moves the blue 'stretcher' bar, which in turn moves the blades.

There are two little notches (grey) in the sleeper under the lever which hold it in place. To change the point the lever is lifted up a little and moved across to the other notch.

It is very important that the point blades do not move when a train is moving over them. This would cause a derailment because one half of the train would go one way and the other half of the train would go the other way!

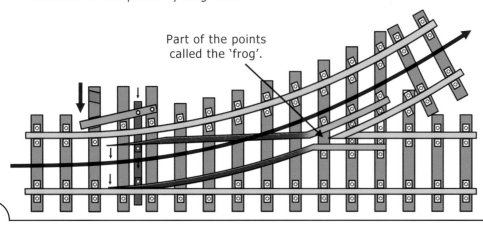

Part of the points called the 'frog'.

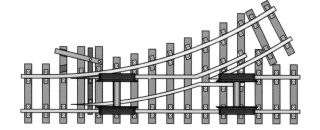

The path that the wheels of the train follow is shown in yellow.

The moving rails or 'blades' guide the wheels straight or onto the curve depending on how the point has been set.

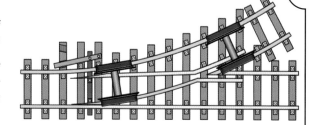

This old photograph of the tracks outside Glasgow Central Station shows how complicated railways can be.

There are lots of sets of points and even a special complicated type called a 'double slip' (in the foreground, just left of centre).

It must have been very difficult for the driver of a train to know which signal on the overhead gantry referred to his track.

On a full size railway the points and signals are usually controlled from a signal box, either by long rods or by electric motors.

SIGNAL GANTRY ON BRIDGE ACROSS RIVER CLYDE, CENTRAL STATION, GLASGOW

(M'Kenzie, Holland, & Westinghouse Power Signal Co., Ltd.)

A Turntable at Eight Elms

The next day, back at the farm, Peter and Grandpa went to look at their railway outside Eight Elms engine shed and beside Gerald's Cross station. They were looking for the best place to build their turntable.

They would have to put in some extra track beside the platform so that they could drive the engine from one end of the train to the other. They could build the turntable in the middle of this track. They would also need to make and install some sets of points to enable the engine to be switched from one track to another.

It was quite difficult to see how it would all fit in.

"If we ran the track through this flowerbed here," said Peter standing in the middle of it, "then it could ....."

"I am not sure that is one of your best ideas," Grandpa stopped him quickly. "Grandma has been pretty good about letting us use the garden for a railway. But digging up her flowerbed would be most unpopular. And anyway it would spoil the look of the station."

"You have just reminded me of a story from the very earliest times of the railways," he continued, as he sat down on the seat on the platform.

"A party of surveyors were trying to find the best route for a railway through a particular piece of countryside. Now this land all belonged to a most unpleasant man who hated the idea of trains going across his fields. So he sent his men out to stop the surveyors from doing their work. The only trouble was that his men entered into the spirit of his instructions rather too well and started firing pot shots at the surveyors with their rifles to try to scare them away."

"Oh dear," said Peter, quickly jumping out of the flower bed. "We don't want Grandma taking pot shots at us from that upstairs bedroom window!"

They looked behind the engine shed, but to make space for the turntable they would have to cut down one of the lovely old elm trees.

"We can't do that," said Grandpa. "There aren't many elm trees left now. Most of them have died out."

"You're quite right, it's a rotten idea anyway," laughed Peter. "If we cut one of them down, we would have to make a new sign for the engine shed saying *Seven* Elms."

Eventually they decided that the best place for the turntable would be at the far end of the station platform and this had another advantage. For very little extra work they could build a short length, or spur of track into Grandpa's workshop. It could go in through the door in the end wall. This would be very useful whenever they wanted to move Fiery Fox or any of the wagons into the workshop for repairs.

Peter did a sketch on a piece of paper to show where the turntable and its tracks would have to go. It would guide them when they were setting it all out on the ground.

The most important thing to decide was how big the turntable should be so that Fiery Fox would fit onto it and turn round without catching on anything.

They went into the engine shed with a tape measure and checked the length of the engine. It was about two and a half metres long but they decided to make the turntable three metres long in case they ever had a larger locomotive running on the railway. It would be a nuisance if they had gone to all the trouble of building a turntable and it wasn't big enough.

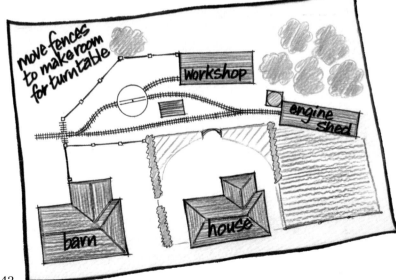

Next they had to decide how they would make the turning part of the whole thing. They would need some sort of very strong bearing for the middle. It would have to support the weight of the track and the locomotive and yet allow it to spin round easily.

As usual when they needed something, the two of them set off for a walk round the farm. Grandpa had piles of "one day this will come in handy" stuff. Building materials, old vehicles, broken machinery, all over the place, just waiting for a new lease of life.

"Look over there," said Grandpa, pointing to an old tractor. "That's a complete wreck as the engine blew up years ago. I should have sent it off for scrap but never got round to it. There are two very strong bearings in the back axle for the rear wheels. One of the wheel hubs with its bearing would be perfect. We would just set it up vertically."

"And if we used some of the big outside casing," Peter said, pointing to a large red bit, "it would make a really good base to hold it all firmly in the ground."

"Well done Peter!" said Grandpa grinning. "We can dig a hole, set the casing down into it and then pour in some concrete to hold it all in place. The only bit sticking up and out of the concrete will be the hub which the wheel used to bolt onto. It will turn very easily but still be plenty strong enough to do what we need."

"Now we need some sort of strong beam to make the swinging part of the turntable," added Grandpa.

They looked all over the farm, trying to find something about three metres long that would be strong enough to hold the engine. Eventually they found an old metal girder which had been left over when Grandpa had built a new barn. It was an off-cut from one of the roof beams. Grandpa had put it to one side, thinking that one day he might have a use for it. He never imagined at the time that it might be made into a turntable for a small steam locomotive! It was a bit longer than necessary but it didn't take long to cut it down to size with an angle grinder.

The first large job was to dig a circular pit in the ground. It had to be three metres in diameter and deep enough to allow the beam of the turntable to swing round. They marked out a circle using a piece of string attached to a peg in the centre, with a stick at the other end to scratch a line in the earth.

It would be very hard work to dig such a large pit by hand so they decided to use Grandpa's old digger. Once they had got it going, with its usual rumble and clouds of smoke, it made light work of the job. They dug the pit out to an even depth and then dug an extra deep hole in the middle to take the back wheel bearing from the old tractor. When it was finished, they built a little brick wall round the inside edge of the pit to stop the sides falling in.

The next day, armed with a jack and some large spanners, Peter and Grandpa set about the old tractor to unbolt the rear wheel bearing and its casing. They had to jack it up and take off the back wheel and then there were lots of bolts which had to be undone. The bearing was perfect and just what they needed. It was heavy so they put it in Grandma's wheel barrow and took it up to their turntable pit.

They put the bearing in the hole and it was time to mix up some concrete.

"We'll need one load to fix the bearing in position," said Grandpa, "and a few more to pour in to make a firm base in the pit. Let's try to get it done today and then it will have all gone solid by tomorrow."

It was hard work mixing it all up, shovelling it in and then spreading it round but they finished before it was dark.

In the morning they had to lift the beam into the pit and bolt it onto the bearing. It was very heavy and would be difficult to move by hand so they used the old digger as a crane. They found some rope and tied it to the digger's shovel and round the beam. Grandpa started it up and with a loud roar and clouds of smoke, the digger lifted the beam up and gently lowered it onto the bearing.

Peter put the bolts through the holes which Grandpa had drilled in the beam and tightened up the nuts with a spanner. It was then only a small job to fix some rails to the top of the beam and they were really making progress.

To finish it off they fitted a sliding bolt so that the turntable could be locked in position. It would be a disaster if the turntable moved when the engine was just crossing the joint between the track on the ground and the track on the turntable. There would be a nasty derailment.

They decided that before they put Fiery Fox onto the new turntable, they had better make sure it was strong enough to hold her weight. It would be terrible if it broke while she was on it; she would be ruined.

"I'll go and get a trailer load of concrete blocks," said Grandpa. "Fiery Fox weighs about 400 kg and we want to test the turntable with at least double that weight to be sure it's safe."

Each block weighed about 10 kg so he fetched 80 of them, making a load of 800 kg; nearly a tonne. Grandpa had quite a few left over from a building project a few years ago and they were always coming in handy for odd jobs.

They loaded the blocks on one by one and held their breath as they lowered the last one into place. There was no need to worry though, the turntable was plenty strong enough.

There was no time to rest though. There was still lots to do to make the sets of points and lay the extra tracks to the turntable. They already had some lengths of track left over from when they built the railway but the points were something new and would need some careful work. They decided to make the set of points for the loop at Woodland Cottage at the same time.

Every evening, Grandpa would disappear into his workshop to get them finished quickly. He had to work very accurately so the trains would run over them smoothly and not derail. He made some special sleepers, all different lengths to hold the rails together. The milling machine was used to make the two special rails which taper down to a thin blade and also to make the special crossing part called the *frog*. There were lots of holes to be drilled so that everything could be bolted together in the correct positions.

Once they were made, it took a few days to lay the track and connect the turntable to the railway and the workshop. Now they could try Fiery Fox on it.

They didn't light the fire and raise steam. They just rolled her out of the shed, set the points to lead her onto the right track and pushed her along and onto the turntable.

"I'll put the hand brake on," said Peter. "We don't want her to roll off the turntable when it's half way round."

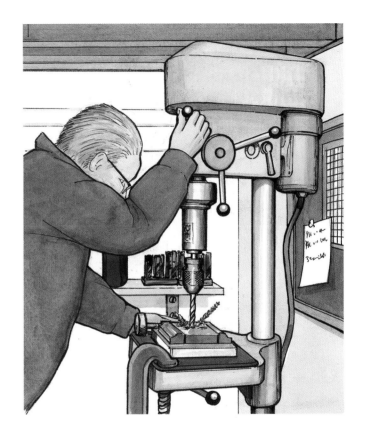

He then pushed gently on the side of the turntable and was amazed at how easily it turned. Once he had got it moving, it carried on turning slowly until he put his hand on it again and stopped it.

"I never expected it to turn as easily as that," he said. "Although that old tractor was a wreck, the bearing is still as good as new."

"Now this all reminds me of an incident I was told about many years ago," Grandpa started. "There was a railway which ran right next to the sea, between the beach and some cliffs. At one of the stations there was a turntable and, because there wasn't a lot of space, the circle of the turntable pit was cut partly into the cliff."

"Well one night," he continued, "there was a tremendous storm and the wind was blowing right along the cliffs. Everything was fine until they put an engine on the turntable and started to swing it around. When it got half way round, the back half of the engine was sheltered in the cut-out of the cliff and the front half was sticking right out in the gale."

"I think I can guess what is coming next," laughed Peter.

"Yes," smiled Grandpa. "The wind caught the engine and gave it a good push and started it spinning faster. Then the front got into the shelter of the cliff and the wind gave another push on the back. No one could stop it. Every time it went round the wind gave it another shove and it got a bit faster. Things were getting quite out of hand!"

"Whatever did they do?" asked Peter. "Did they just leave it spinning and wait for the wind to die down?"

"No, it was much too dangerous to leave it like that," said Grandpa. "Luckily the driver kept his head and very carefully drove the engine forward a fraction so that the whole turntable was not quite so well balanced. The extra bit of friction eventually slowed it down until they could get it under control again."

"I would love to have seen it," said Peter laughing. "It must have looked very funny with the engine spinning round and round and everyone in a panic, wondering what to do about it!"

"Would you like to have a steam up tomorrow?" Grandpa offered when they had stopped laughing. "You could start learning to drive Fiery Fox."

"That's a brilliant idea," said Peter, "but I think we had better make a start on building the loop at Woodland Cottage. I am afraid that once I get started driving, we will never get around to building the loop line. Let's do that tomorrow instead."

The Turntable

This is a view of the turntable from above, sometimes called a 'plan' view.

The piece of track which rotates to turn the locomotive is set on the beam (green). The short lengths of track are just the ends of the lines or 'roads' which lead to and from the turntable.

The beam turns on a very strong bearing which was rescued from a broken old tractor. The bearing was a part of the back axle and is not visible in this view because it is underneath the beam. A dotted circle indicates where it is. The six nuts (pink) which hold the beam to the hub are visible in the centre.

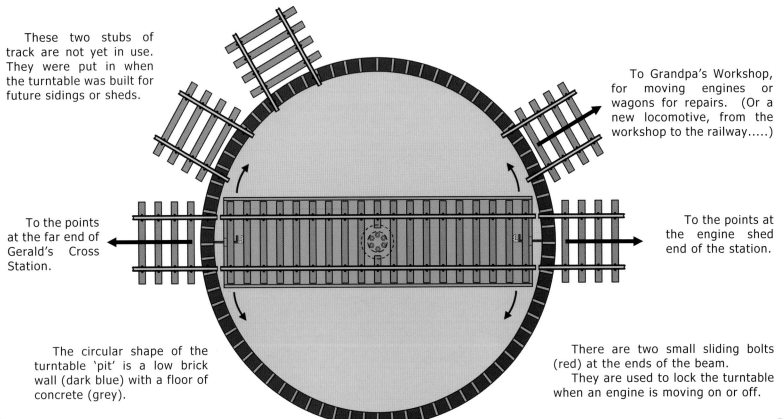

These two stubs of track are not yet in use. They were put in when the turntable was built for future sidings or sheds.

To Grandpa's Workshop, for moving engines or wagons for repairs. (Or a new locomotive, from the workshop to the railway.....)

To the points at the far end of Gerald's Cross Station.

To the points at the engine shed end of the station.

The circular shape of the turntable 'pit' is a low brick wall (dark blue) with a floor of concrete (grey).

There are two small sliding bolts (red) at the ends of the beam.

They are used to lock the turntable when an engine is moving on or off.

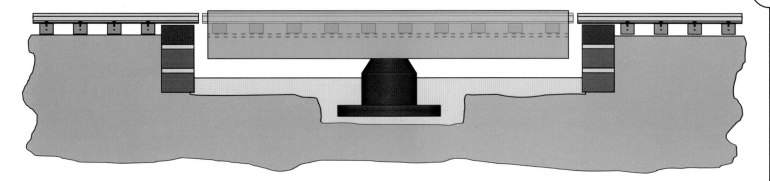

This is a view of the turntable looking from the side. It is called a 'section' or 'sectional view' because it shows a cross section of the turntable. It is like a slice through the middle.

The 'pit' is shown dug into the earth (brown) with the concrete floor (grey). Around the edge of the pit is a low brick retaining wall to keep the earth from falling in. The rotating beam (green) is clearly shown supported on the old tractor back axle and bearing (red). The casing of the bearing can be seen set deeply into the concrete to hold it solidly.

Two rows of bricks in the retaining wall are of the ordinary type (reddish/orange), the top row are dark blue, almost black. These are known as Engineers' Blues and are extra strong. Engineers' Blues are used when ordinary bricks would crumble and they can be seen in many railway bridges and structures where very high strength is needed.

This is a view looking along the beam of the turntable. Some of the ground and the brick wall have been cut away to make it clear.

The beam (green) is known as an 'I' beam because of its shape. In this case it is an 'I' lying on its side.

The hub (blue) of the back axle is bolted very solidly to the beam with nuts and bolts (pink). The back wheel of the tractor used to be bolted to this hub.

The track is fixed to the top of the beam with the end view of the rails shown in yellow.

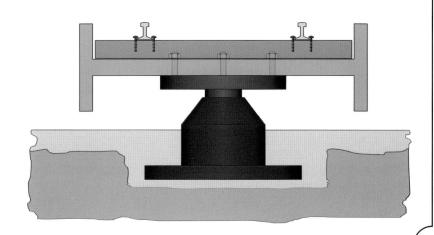

Plain Bearings and Ball Bearings
How do shafts and axles in machines turn easily?

When a shaft or axle in a machine needs to turn freely, a bearing is needed.

The bearing needs to be able to carry the necessary load, turn very easily and last a long time. Some shafts spin very fast and the bearing will need to work at high speed.

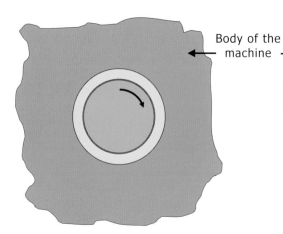

Body of the machine ←

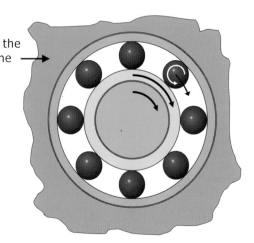

Plain Bearing

The shaft (green) which needs to spin freely is a close sliding fit in a metal sleeve bearing or 'bush' (yellow). The bearing is often made of brass or bronze.

Oil is supplied to the very small gap between the shaft and the bearing to reduce friction and to give the bearing a long working life.

A plain bearing is sometimes called a 'journal' bearing. They are often used for crankshafts and the 'big end' bearings of connecting rods.

Ball Bearing

A ball bearing consists of two metal rings or 'races' (pale blue and pink) and a set of balls (red).

As the shaft (green) rotates, the inner race (pale blue) turns with it and rolls around on the balls.

The balls roll round the inside of the outer race (pink).

The inner race is a tight fit on the shaft and the outer race is a tight fit into the machine so that they do not slip round.

The rolling action has very low friction.

Ball Bearing (cut-away)

This is a photograph of a ball bearing with a section of the outer race cut away so you can see inside.

The two races have a groove running round them which make tracks for the balls to roll in.

The balls sit in a cage to keep them spaced out from each other.

Oil or grease is used to lubricate the bearing.

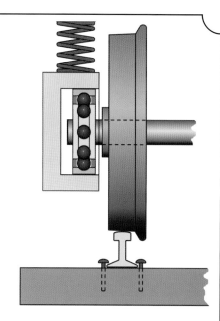

Ball Bearing (Open type)

There are lots of advantages in using a ball bearing instead of a plain bearing. Ball bearings:

1 Are cheap.
2 Usually last longer than plain bearings.
3 Can operate at very high speeds.
4 Need no maintenance until they wear out or break.
5 Are easy to replace when they do wear out.

This open type of ball bearing would be lubricated by oil or grease inside the machine. The machine will have seals to keep the oil in and the dirt out.

Puzzle !

See if you can think how it is possible to put this bearing together from its different parts.

It is not at all obvious how you get the balls into the space between the races and into their grooves.

The answer is somewhere in this book.........

Ball Bearing (Sealed type)

This is a photograph of one of the ball bearings used on the axles of the wagons on Peter's Railway. (Only 25 mm across.)

This type of bearing is sealed for life. The blue seals (one on each side) keep the oil or grease inside the bearing and also keep dirt out.

They are very useful in parts of machines which are outside or operate in dirty places.

A really big advantage is that there is no need to provide any means of lubrication as it is a part of the bearing.

Here is a familiar application for ball bearings: The hub of a bicycle wheel.

This is a sealed bearing (black seals this time) so it never needs oiling and the dirt doesn't get in to damage it.

You can see the axle in the middle, then the shiny inner race. Next is the black rubber seal and then the shiny outer race. All of this is mounted in the hub of the wheel.

This diagram shows how a ball bearing is used on the axles of the railway wagons.

The bearing is a snug fit in the axlebox (grey) and a snug fit on the axle (green).

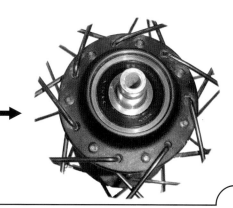

Looping the Loop and Learning to Drive

Peter and Grandpa spent the next couple of weeks building the loop line at Woodland Cottage. Luckily there was plenty of space in the orchard behind the house and it was quite a simple job because the ground was almost perfectly flat.

They had all the materials they needed. There were some rails and sleepers left over from the original railway and Grandpa had made a superb job of constructing the points. There was still quite a pile of ballast stones to make the base for the track panels to bed down into.

They also used their old method of transporting all the materials to the site by rail. The ballast was loaded into the special wagon with a door in the end and two flat wagons carried new lengths of track. It did not take long to empty the ballast out of the wagon, rake it flat and bolt the new length of track into place. A bit of work with a spirit level and pushing the ballast under or away from the track soon had it nice and level and they could get to work on the next length.

The loop was now finished and Peter was up at the farm. He and Grandpa were walking along the track pulling up some weeds which had just appeared.

This afternoon they were going to raise steam in Fiery Fox to test out the loop and turntable. For the first time they would be able to drive the train with the locomotive always facing forwards.

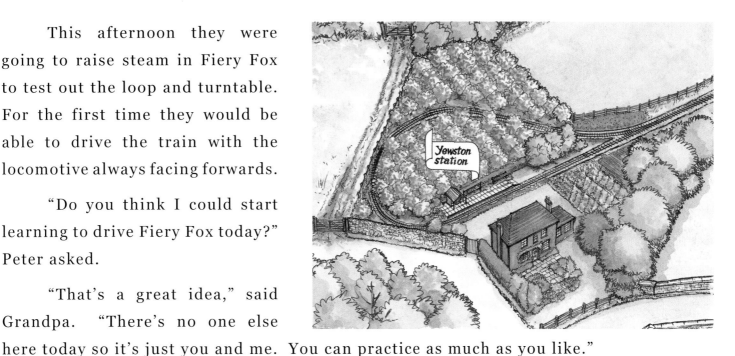

"Do you think I could start learning to drive Fiery Fox today?" Peter asked.

"That's a great idea," said Grandpa. "There's no one else here today so it's just you and me. You can practice as much as you like."

Peter could hardly eat lunch, he was much too excited! But when finished, they went to the engine shed and started to get ready. Peter checked there was plenty of water in the boiler and then filled up the tender with coal and water so they wouldn't run out.

He put a firelighter and some charcoal into the firebox and then came the great moment. It was time to light up. He stuck a match and held it to the firelighter. It lit easily and soon had the charcoal burning too. Smoke started to drift up out of the chimney. Once the flames were flickering brightly, Peter added the first few shovelfuls of coal onto the fire. It was important to add the coal little by little until the fire was really hot or it could easily be smothered and put out. It didn't take long for the fire to start burning well and soon the boiler was getting nice and hot. It was quiet in the shed and they could hear it starting to sing like an old fashioned kettle, sizzling away to itself.

While the boiler was heating up and they were waiting for the steam pressure to rise, Peter started to oil all of the moving parts of the engine. This would help it run smoothly and make sure it did not wear itself out. He had memorized where all the little oil cups and tanks were and counted them off as he filled each one. The oil cups were mounted on parts of the motion and oiled a single joint. The oil tanks being rather bigger, were mounted on the running plate beside the boiler and had lots of little pipes running from underneath to the different places which needed lubricating.

Once everything was oiled and while they were still waiting for the steam pressure to come up, Grandpa told Peter about the main controls in the cab, in case he had forgotten anything important.

The first one was the main steam valve or regulator. "It controls the flow of steam from the boiler to the cylinders," explained Grandpa. "The more you open it the faster you will go. Or more importantly, if you find you are going too fast, just close it a little and the engine will start to slow down."

"This handle is the reverser; you turn it to control the valves on the cylinders. The little indicator on the top shows if they are set for forward running or reverse. When you leave the locomotive it's important to turn the reverser till the indicator is in the middle. Then if someone opens the regulator by mistake, the engine won't move and run away."

"The brakes will probably take some getting used to," said Grandpa. "They take a little while to work after you move the lever. And once they are on, they take a little while to release when you put the lever back to the off position."

They checked the glass water gauge on the boiler to

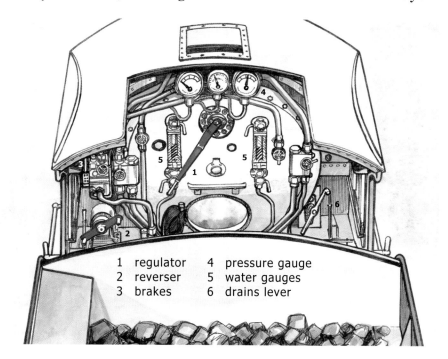

1	regulator	4	pressure gauge
2	reverser	5	water gauges
3	brakes	6	drains lever

make sure the water level was still safe and saw that the pressure gauge was creeping up. It wouldn't be long before they had a full head of steam.

Every few minutes Peter put a few more shovelfuls of coal on the fire. It was getting really hot now and he could feel the heat on his hand every time he opened the firehole door.

"I think the best thing for your first few drives," continued Grandpa, "is just to concentrate on the regulator, reverser and brakes. Don't worry about the water level and the fire while you are driving, there won't be a problem on a single run and we can check to make sure all is correct when we stop at the stations.

"Will I have to use the cylinder drain valves like Dave did on Green Goddess?" asked Peter.

"I think you had better," replied Grandpa. "You won't forget to close them because there will be clouds of steam to remind you they are open. Just remember when you stop to leave them open, ready for the start of the next run."

Peter sat on the little seat on Fiery Fox's tender and checked the water level. It was fine, so he put on a few shovelfuls of coal to make sure he didn't lose steam pressure.

Finally Grandpa sat down on one of the wagons and they were ready.

This was the moment that Peter had been waiting for since they first started building the railway. He was so excited he could hardly wait to go. At the same time he wanted to be very careful so that he did not make any terrible mistakes.

Peter's expression was a mixture of total concentration and excitement.

He checked that the cylinder drains were open, wound the reverser into full forward gear, took the brakes off and very gently opened the regulator.

Fiery Fox pulled slowly out of the shed and into the bright sunlight in a cloud of steam from the drains. There were no passengers to pick up today so he steamed straight through the station and out onto the main line across the farm.

The cylinders were warming up nicely now so he shut the drains and opened the regulator a bit more. This was his first ever drive to Woodland Cottage and Yewston station at the other end of the railway.

Peter was concentrating like mad on driving the engine and looking out for any obstructions on the line like sticks from trees or wandering sheep. Anyone watching would have seen he had a grin as wide as his face.

They had left the garden, farmyard and pond behind them and were now crossing the meadow with Grandpa's cows. Most of them had got quite used to trains rolling across their field and just carried on eating the grass. One of them however always trotted over to inspect the passing train.

Grandpa used to call her Curly because of her rough coat of fur, but recently they had changed her name to *The Engineer*!

Leaving the meadow and The Engineer behind them, the train went though a gap in the hedge and into Bluebell Wood. Peter eased back the regulator to lower the speed a little because of all the bends in the track as it wound its way around the old trees. But just before leaving the wood, the track started to climb on a gentle rising gradient and he found that he had to open the regulator quite a lot to keep the train going at a good pace.

Crossing the next field, the line was on a gently falling gradient and Peter had to shut off steam a little so as not to go too fast. They were now on an embankment and heading towards the river. It was a lovely scene with the waterfall and trees but he had to start to think about slowing down for the end of the run at Yewston station.

He shut off steam completely and pulled the brake lever towards him. At first nothing happened and he hoped it wasn't broken. Then little by little he could feel the brakes going on and the train slowing down.

Oops! He had slightly overdone it and he had to release the brakes and open the regulator a fraction. Fiery Fox pulled gently on the train and they glided into the station. At the last moment Peter shut the regulator and applied the brakes. They stopped with the locomotive right at the end of the platform. Perfect.

"Did I do okay Grandpa?" he asked.

"Well I was a bit worried at first," admitted Grandpa. "But once I realized that you were completely in control of things and weren't going to drive like a maniac, I just settled down to enjoy the ride. In fact I was so relaxed that I lay down flat on the wagon and enjoyed the view. It's the first time I haven't been busy driving so I could really look around."

Peter checked the water level and decided he should put some more in the boiler. He opened the water valve and then the steam valve for the injector.

The injector is a cunning gadget which uses steam from the boiler to inject more water into it from the tender. Peter had been shown how to use it the last time they had the engine running.

Putting the cold water into the boiler had reduced the steam pressure a little so Peter put some more coal on the fire to bring it up again. After a short wait all was back in order and he was ready for the return trip.

It was very pleasant sitting on the platform at their station in the garden at Woodland Cottage but Peter wanted to do some more engine driving.

"Just remember to take it steady on the loop as this is the first train on it," reminded Grandpa.

For the first time they set off forwards from Yewston station, going beyond it and onto their new loop. The line ran round the orchard and turned back on itself to join the old track on the other side of the station. There was no need to set the points as they are the sprung type and the locomotive just pushed them over to cross onto the main line.

Peter drove back to the farm at a nice and easy speed. Nothing special and not too fast.

When they got back to Gerald's Cross there was another interest for them. They could turn Fiery Fox on the turntable ready for the next run.

Peter uncoupled the engine from the train, ran it forward over the points and then set them over the other way with the lever. He then gently reversed Fiery Fox along beside the train, past Grandpa's workshop and onto the turntable.

He slid the bolt to unlock the turntable, turned the engine round and then locked it in position again, ready to drive the engine off. This time he drove the engine to the other end of the platform, ready for the run back to Woodland Cottage.

"You are doing well," said Grandpa when they stopped for a rest. "Now for the really difficult part. You can try putting on water and coal while you are on the move. That will keep you busy!"

On the next run, when they arrived at Yewston station, instead of stopping as usual, Peter ran straight on through and round the loop for the return run to the farm. Working the injector to put water in the boiler was not too difficult, but trying to get the coal through the firehole door when everything was swaying around with the motion of the train was much trickier. He put more on the floor of the cab than in the fire.

They spent the rest of the afternoon driving up and down the railway, with Peter getting more and more skilful each time.

On one run, just as the train was pulling out of the station, Minnie ran across the garden and jumped onto one of the wagons and came for the ride. All the way to Woodland Cottage and back again.

"Minnie riding on the train like that reminds me of a story," remembered Grandpa. "Many years ago on the Great Western Railway, there was a dog known as Station Jim. He lived at Slough station and wore a collecting box on his back. Whenever someone put some coins in the box he would bark to say thank you. The money he collected was used to look after old ladies and children who needed help. Sometimes Jim would jump on a train and go for an adventure. He always seemed to know exactly where he was going and never seemed to get lost."

"Nowadays," Grandpa sighed, "the only collecting dogs you see are horrible plastic things with a slot in the top of their heads. Not the same thing at all really."

After a few more runs they finally stopped for a cup of tea and biscuits with Grandma at the farm.

"I have learnt a lot this afternoon," Peter said happily. "It's a pity that lessons at school aren't as much fun as this!"

"Just to bring you two back to earth for a minute," said Grandma. "Don't forget that I am going away for a few days to visit old Aunt Ethel. I wonder if I might ask you to do a little job for me while I'm away?"

"Of course," they both replied. "What is it?"

"I have bought some lovely bright blue paint," said Grandma. "I thought it would make the sitting room look much more cheerful than the rather grubby white it is now. Would you two paint the room while I am away?"

Grandpa and Peter glanced at each other. Neither of them much liked decorating rooms. It wasn't much fun and it would keep them indoors for most of the two days. However they didn't like to refuse because Grandma did so much for them.

"Of course we will," said Grandpa. "It will be done by the time you get home."

He had a great idea to speed the job up................

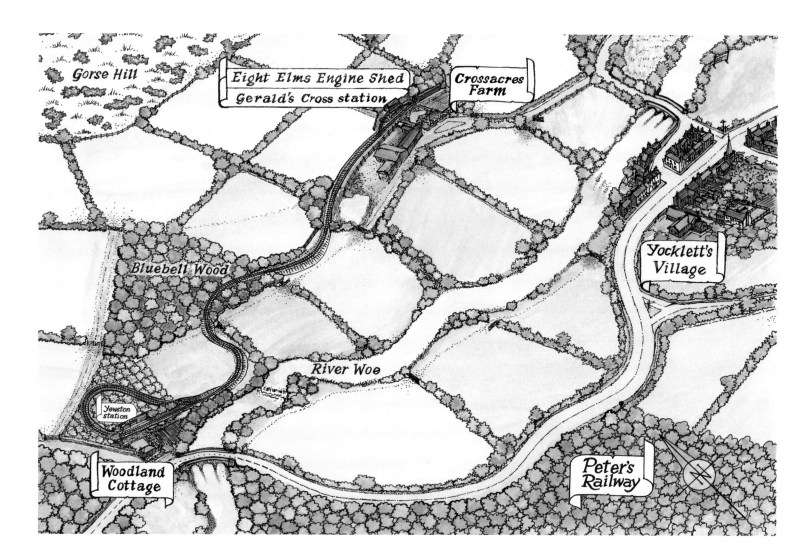

Gorse Hill

Eight Elms Engine Shed

Gerald's Cross station

Crossacres Farm

Bluebell Wood

Yocklett's Village

River Woe

Yewston station

Woodland Cottage

Peter's Railway

Page 69

Girls Like Trains Too!

Macy admires a locomotive at the Romney Hythe and Dymchurch Railway.
Photograph by Tony Crowhurst.

Turning Loop and Sprung Point

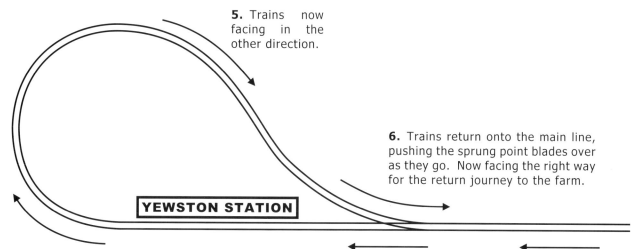

5. Trains now facing in the other direction.

6. Trains return onto the main line, pushing the sprung point blades over as they go. Now facing the right way for the return journey to the farm.

YEWSTON STATION

4. Trains leave the station and run onto the turning loop.

3. Trains arrive at Yewston Station for Woodland Cottage.

2. The spring holds the points to the straight through position.

1. Trains arrive from Gerald's Cross Station at the other end of the line.

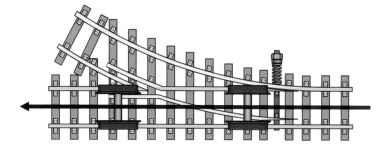

Arriving at the sprung points, the train is guided to the station. The spring holds the points in the straight through position.

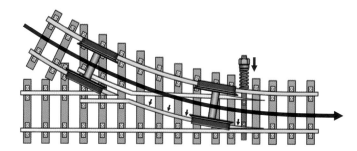

When returning from the loop to join the main line again, the wheels of the train push against the blades of the points. The blades can be pushed over because the spring can be squashed a little.

How (not) to Paint a Sitting Room

All was quiet the next day at Crossacres Farm. Grandma had just gone away to visit her old aunt and Peter and Grandpa were busy pulling up more weeds on the railway.

"You know how Grandma asked us to paint the sitting room for her?" said Grandpa. "Well I've got an idea which would speed the job up and get it done in the blink of an eye."

"That sounds like one of your cunning plans," said Peter, looking intrigued. "How will we paint it so quickly?"

"Well," said Grandpa, "a long time ago I read about a method for painting large factories when they are empty. What they do is to place a container of paint right in the middle and then set off a small explosive charge like a big banger in the middle of the paint. The idea is that the explosion blows open the container and then blasts the paint all over the place. The walls, floor and ceiling are all painted in an instant."

"I have never seen it done," he went on, "but I wonder if we might get it to work and get the sitting room painted before Grandma gets home?"

Peter thought the whole scheme sounded rather dodgy, but it also sounds like a lot of fun and much better than spending two days inside with a paint brush.

It also seemed a shame to spoil the fun by alerting Grandpa to all the obvious dangers of his madcap plan. So he agreed they should give it a try.

The first thing to do was to find some sort of container for the blue paint. It must obviously be water (or paint) proof, but it must also be weak enough so that it would blow to bits and not hold onto the paint.

"I've got it," said Peter after a bit of thinking. "Why don't we use a plastic carrier bag? We could hang it from the light in the centre of the ceiling."

"Brilliant!" said Grandpa. "And I know what we can use as the explosive. I've got some bangers for scaring birds off the fields. They go off with the most terrific bang and have a nice slow burning fuse. We can light one and retire to a safe place before it blows up.

I think one should be powerful enough to blast the paint about, without blowing up the house as that would be a major mistake."

Our two heroes then carried all the furniture out of the room and covered the carpet with lots of old newspapers as Grandma had not made any mention of painting the floor.

Next they poured the new paint into a carrier bag and very carefully tied it with a piece of string to the light in the middle of the room.

"Hang on a minute," laughed Peter. "There's something we've forgotten. If we don't open the windows they will get painted blue or we might even blow out all the glass."

They were ready. The paint was hanging in the bag, the carpet was covered up and the windows were wide open.

"Just think," said Grandpa winking at Peter. "The whole room will be painted in a *flash*." And he threw open his arms in a most dramatic gesture. "*Flash* Peter. Get it?"

"*Grandpa*," groaned Peter, "I hope this scheme of yours is better than your jokes!"

"I have every confidence in it," said Grandpa boldly. "Just think how pleased Grandma will be when she gets home and finds it all painted blue."

"Mind you," he added, "I think it's a good thing she isn't here to see how we are going to do it. She would take rather a dim view of it all I suspect."

Peter thought that Grandma would take more than just a dim view of Grandpa painting her sitting room with a small bomb. But he simply agreed about how pleased she would be to see the result.

Grandpa lit the fuse on the bird scarer, dropped it into the bag of paint and they both left the room quickly, shutting the door behind them. (Grandma had wanted the inside of that painted as well.)

They waited in the kitchen for the bang…….

Unfortunately they heard three sounds in quick succession: First was the terrific bang followed immediately by a very loud 'Miaooww'. After that was the sound of Grandma's car coming up the road.

"Oh Dear!" said Peter. "Cato must have jumped in through the open window. The bang must have given him an awful fright."

"Let's at least hope it has worked," said Grandpa with a worried look on his face. "I have a feeling I am going to be in trouble."

Just then Grandma ran into the kitchen.

"Er, hello Dear," spluttered Grandpa. "We weren't expecting you back just yet…."

"Never mind about that," said Grandma crossly. "I was driving up the road when I heard a loud bang and then Cato leapt out of the sitting room window at about a hundred miles an hour. And the whole of one side of him was painted bright blue!"

"Whatever have you done?" she demanded, opening the sitting room door and running in. Peter and Grandpa followed quickly behind her.

Everything was blue. The ceiling, the light switch (and light bulb), the skirting boards and the walls were all perfectly painted blue. Except that is, for one part of one wall which had a large patch which was still white. It was a perfect shadow of Cato.

"I wanted it to be a surprise for you when you got home Dear," said Grandpa, rather lamely.

"Well it was certainly a surprise for poor Cato," muttered Grandma. "It's just as well I was only away for two days. Goodness knows what you two would get up to if I went away for any longer."

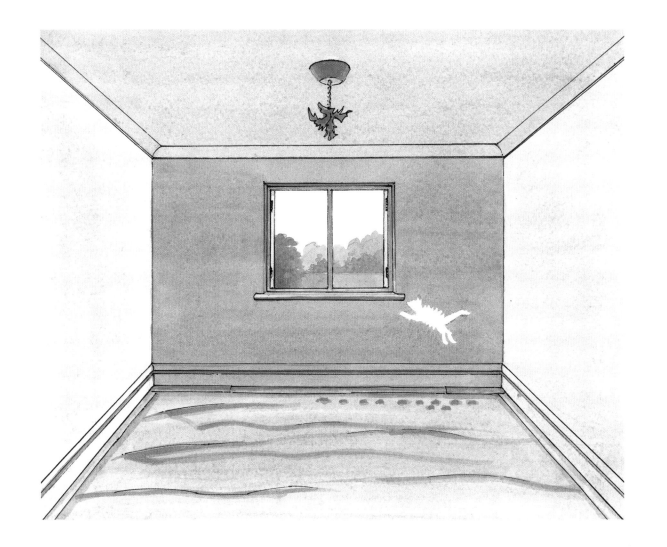

The Moonlight Express

A few days later everything was back to normal at Crossacres Farm. Grandpa had been forgiven for his painting experiment and Cato had been out in the rain and all the paint had washed off.

Amazingly Grandma had decided that the shadow painting of Cato on the wall should be left as a permanent reminder of one of Grandpa's less successful schemes.

It was her birthday very soon and Peter and Grandpa were in the sitting room, trying to decide how to celebrate it or what to get her as a present.

"Paint another room for her?" suggested Peter mischievously.

But then he had a proper idea.

"We could give her a good birthday dinner down at Woodland Cottage," he suggested. "I am sure Mum would be happy to cook for us all and we could use the train to bring Grandma over to the house and back again so that she doesn't have to drive. And I could stay the night at the farm afterwards."

"That's a great idea," said Grandpa smiling. "We won't tell her and then it will be a surprise party. We will have to think up some excuse to get her to come for a ride in the Granny Wagon as it would be a shame if she refused to go to her own party."

"If we call it the Granny Wagon she will certainly refuse to go in it," giggled Peter. "We'll have to remember to call it her *Great Western* Saloon Coach."

They decided that on the day of her birthday, they would ask her to come for a ride in her saloon coach. She could inspect the work they had done at the far end of the railway and also see how well Peter has learnt to drive the locomotive.

Because it would be dark after the party, there were a few preparations they had to make for the return journey.

First they would need a small torch so that Peter could see the water and pressure gauges in the cab. He also wondered if they should have a headlamp for the locomotive and Grandpa agreed. A small lamp on the front would make Fiery Fox look most realistic in the dark.

"What we do need though," said Grandpa, "is some sort of light beside the track to tell us when we are getting close to arriving at Gerald's Cross station. It's so dark in the countryside at night that we might not realize we are at the end of the line. Then we would smash into the buffers in the engine shed. I don't think Grandma would want to be in a train crash on her birthday!"

After a bit of rummaging around in his workshop Grandpa found what he was looking for. It was an old oil lamp which he had been given by a retired railwayman. It burned for many hours on one filling of oil and could be set to three different colours: White, green and red.

"We will set it to red and leave it beside the track just near the duck pond," said Grandpa. "When you see the red glow in the dark you will have plenty of time to slow down for the station."

A few days later it was Grandma's birthday. Peter's Mum, Jo, had spent a lot of time getting ready for the party and as a bonus it was a really nice clear and sunny day.

After lunch Peter and Grandpa went out to the engine shed to get everything ready. They polished up all the paint and brass work on Fiery Fox until it gleamed. Next they gave the Granny Wagon a really good clean on the inside and a polish on the outside. It looked splendid.

The last job to prepare for Grandma's inspection of the line was to fill her carriage lamp with oil and put some dry wood in the stove for later. They still had lots of the off-cuts from when they had made all the sleepers, so it would not be too expensive to keep Grandma warm.

Although they didn't want to use the engine just yet, they lit the fire early so that it would be ready with plenty of steam for when they needed it.

"Grandma?" asked Peter at tea time. "Would you do us the honour of inspecting the railway from your Saloon Carriage?"

"Oh I don't know," said Grandma. "I think I'm getting a bit too old for riding around on trains."

"Oh please," said Peter. "We've done such a lot of work improving it and I've learnt to drive the engine as well."

"Oh alright," she chuckled. "It does sound awfully grand. An *Inspection* from my *Saloon Carriage*! How could I refuse?"

They all went outside to the station where the train was waiting for her, glinting in the sun.

Peter climbed onto Fiery Fox and checked that everything was in good order for the journey. There was plenty of water in the boiler, the tank in the tender was full too and the fire was burning well. The steam pressure gauge showed one hundred pounds per square inch. He was ready.

Grandpa went off to find Cato and Minnie as they never liked to miss a party. There was always the chance that someone would drop some tasty bits of food on the floor which they could then 'Hoover' up before anyone noticed. He put them in their special wagons and got on the train himself.

Everything was set.

Peter blew the whistle, gently opened the regulator and they steamed off down the line. He drove very slowly because it was meant to be an inspection of the railway. Grandma wouldn't be able to see very much if they whizzed along at high speed.

'One day,' he thought to himself, 'I would love to drive the train really fast.....'

They went past the duck pond where the red light was glowing and then out onto the embankment just before Bluebell Wood. There was a spectacular view from the top. You could see across the fields to the river and beyond to Yockletts village in the distance.

Once clear of the wood, the railway went through some cuttings and onto another embankment as it dropped on a gentle gradient down towards the river bank.

Peter had to ease the regulator back to keep the speed down. He wanted Grandma to be able to enjoy the view.

Finally they arrived at Yewston station in the garden at Woodland Cottage. They all got off the train and Grandma was very surprised to find all the family waiting on the platform. Peter's Mum and Dad, Jo and Colin were there with the twins, Kitty and Harry. Then there was Aunt Ethel and Mr and Mrs Esmond who had become good friends since the arrival of the railway. Also staying for a few days was Peter's Uncle John. Uncle John was a great favourite of Peter's and always explained how everything worked. Most adults can't be bothered to answer endless questions of 'why, how and what for?', but Uncle John always explained everything very patiently and carefully.

"Happy Birthday Grandma!" they all shouted together.

Grandma was tickled pink. (One of her old fashioned expressions.)

"Good gracious, a party." she laughed. "You could knock me down with a feather!" (That was another one of her funny sayings.)

Jo had cooked everyone a huge meal and they all ate far too much.

While they were eating, Peter nipped out through the back door every quarter of an hour to check that everything was alright with Fiery Fox. It wouldn't do to find the fire had gone out when it was time for the return journey to the farm. Even worse would be if the fire was burning well and the water level got low in the boiler. An explosion would definitely spoil the party.

On one of his trips outside, he found both Minnie and Cato had jumped up on the kitchen table and were demolishing what was left of the meat. His Mum had left it out, forgetting what they were like.

On another trip outside he lit the lamp and stove in the Granny Wagon. As he had already put a firelighter under the wood it only took one match and the stove was burning merrily in a few minutes. It would be nice and warm for when Grandma needed it.

At last the party was over and it was time to take Grandma home to the farm.

When everyone was safely on the train, Peter drove the locomotive very carefully out of the station, slowly round the loop in the orchard and then back onto the main line.

It was a dark but clear night. The moon and stars were out and Peter's face was lit up by the fire whenever he opened the door to put more coal on.

Fiery Fox was running perfectly as usual, pulling the train with hardly a sound save the clickety click of the wheels and the chuffs from the chimney.

When he got to the beginning of the gradient, going up this time, he opened the regulator to let a bit more steam into the cylinders. He felt her start to pull on the train more urgently and the chuffs became much louder.

Looking up he noticed that the stars were sometimes visible and then they seemed to go out. But then he realized that it was just the steam and smoke going over his head which were playing tricks on him.

Apart from the light of the moon and stars, it was pitch black.

Suddenly he saw the red glow from the lamp they had left beside the track near the duck pond. It was time to put the brakes on and start slowing down for the station.

It wasn't easy to judge the distance in the dark but he got it correct and stopped with the train right at the platform.

Now that the train was quiet they could all hear a strange rattling sound from Grandma's Saloon. Whatever was it?

Peter opened the door and found that she had fallen fast asleep and was snoring like a motor bike. He gently woke her up and helped her out onto the platform.

"Thank you Peter," she said. "You drove the train so smoothly that I fell fast asleep. I really am most proud of you."

Grandma then went inside to make one last cup of tea for them all, while Peter and Grandpa put the engine to bed in Eight Elms Shed and made sure all was safe.

Chatting over their tea, Grandma said she enjoyed going on the railway so much now that it was a pity that it didn't go to Yockletts village. Then she could use it to do the shopping and Peter and his friends could use it to get to school.

"Now there's a thought for our next project," exclaimed Peter. "How about it Grandpa? The *Yockletts Extension*. Could we build it?"

"As long as you help me Peter," he laughed. "It's a deal!"

Peter went to bed at the farm that night, feeling tired but happy. He fell asleep the moment his head touched the pillow and he dreamt of driving Fiery Fox flat out at night, racing across the fields under the moon and stars.

But that is another story........

The end.

Pistons and Cylinders
How the steam turns the wheels and drives the locomotive

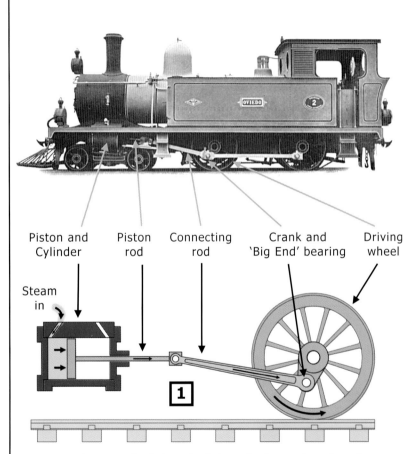

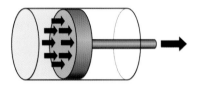

Steam presses on a round piston which is a close sliding fit in the cylinder (a round tube).

The piston and its rod push on the connecting rod which pushes the wheels round. The connecting rod turns the wheels by pushing on a crank, just like a bicycle pedal.

The steam comes from the boiler and is at very high pressure so that it pushes the piston with great force. This is why steam locomotives are so powerful.

Piston and Cylinder   Piston rod   Connecting rod   Crank and 'Big End' bearing   Driving wheel

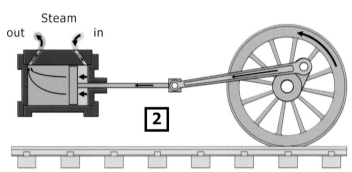

Steam in

Steam out   Steam in

1

2

Steam is let into the left end of the cylinder and pushes the piston to the right, turning the wheel.

Now steam is let into the other end of the cylinder and pushes the piston to the left. The piston is now pulling the connecting rod to pull the wheel round in the same direction. The first lot of steam is being let out as exhaust.

Pistons Rings
How the piston makes a perfect seal with the cylinder

It is important that the piston makes a perfect seal with the cylinder so that the steam does not just leak past it and go to waste up the chimney.

The sealing is done using a 'piston ring' or several of them.

The piston ring is a simple ring of springy metal with a gap.

It is a little larger than the hole or 'bore' of the cylinder in which it will fit.

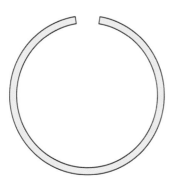

When the piston ring is squeezed inwards and fitted in the cylinder, it presses outwards onto the cylinder wall and makes a perfect seal.

Because it is springy it can follow any unevenness in the cylinder wall and still make a good seal.

The gap is now very small.

A piston designed to use piston rings has grooves to hold the rings.

Two rings will be fitted to this piston.

The rings are shown here fitted to the piston but before they have been squeezed inwards. The large gap is visible on one ring.

The gap on the other ring is on the opposite side of the piston, out of sight.

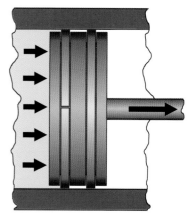

The high pressure steam is pushing against the piston. The rings stop it from leaking past.

It does not matter if the piston is not a very snug fit in the cylinder because the rings do all of the sealing.

Valves
How they control the steam to push the pistons back and forward

In a locomotive, the steam pushes on the piston, first one way and then the other, to turn the wheels. This cycle carries on as long as the driver keeps the main steam valve or 'regulator' open to keep the train moving.

After the steam has done its work in one end of the cylinder, pushing the piston one way, it must be let out again when the piston moves the other way. It is let out to exhaust up the chimney (making the well known chuffing sound).

A clever valve (green) controls the steam so that it is always being let in at the correct end of the cylinder to push the piston. At the same time, the exhaust steam in the other end of the cylinder is being let out to exhaust up the chimney.

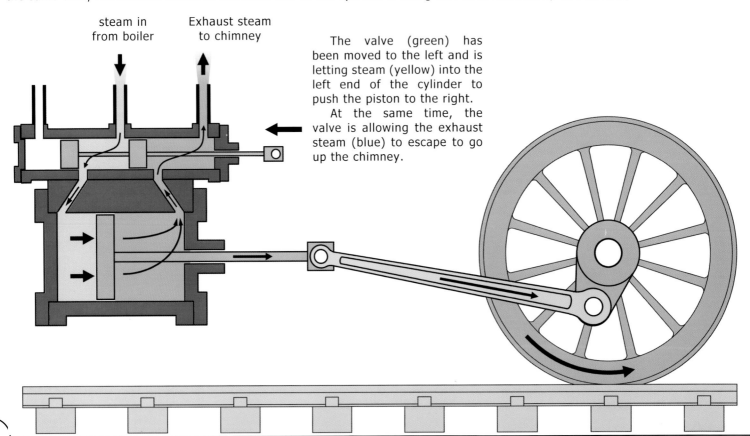

steam in from boiler

Exhaust steam to chimney

The valve (green) has been moved to the left and is letting steam (yellow) into the left end of the cylinder to push the piston to the right.

At the same time, the valve is allowing the exhaust steam (blue) to escape to go up the chimney.

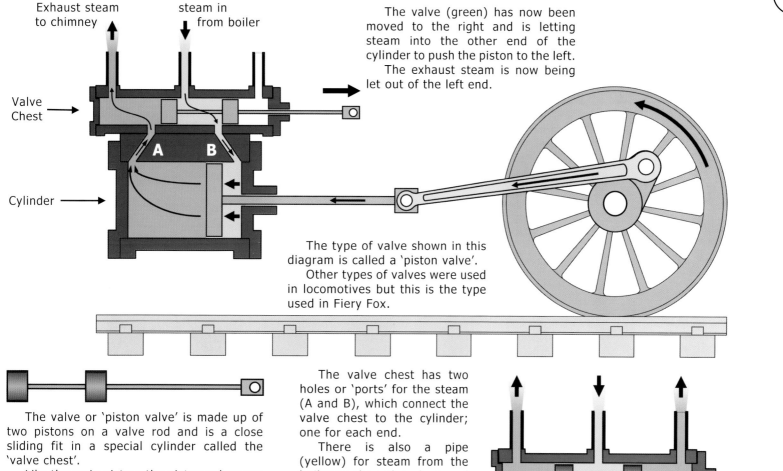

Exhaust steam to chimney

steam in from boiler

Valve Chest

Cylinder

A **B**

The valve (green) has now been moved to the right and is letting steam into the other end of the cylinder to push the piston to the left.

The exhaust steam is now being let out of the left end.

The type of valve shown in this diagram is called a 'piston valve'.

Other types of valves were used in locomotives but this is the type used in Fiery Fox.

The valve or 'piston valve' is made up of two pistons on a valve rod and is a close sliding fit in a special cylinder called the 'valve chest'.

Like the main piston, the piston valves are sealed in their cylinders with piston rings so that precious steam is not wasted by leaking.

The valve is moved by a clever mechanism called the 'valve gear' which makes the movement of the valve automatic.

The valve chest has two holes or 'ports' for the steam (A and B), which connect the valve chest to the cylinder; one for each end.

There is also a pipe (yellow) for steam from the boiler to the valve chest and two pipes (blue) which take exhaust steam to the chimney.

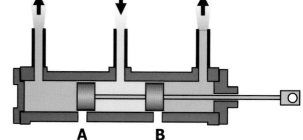

A   **B**

As the valve moves it covers or uncovers the two ports A and B, allowing steam to flow from the boiler to one end of the cylinder and exhaust from the other end of the cylinder to the chimney.

Here the valve is shown in the mid position with both ports closed.

Some Special Words

Ball bearing Type of bearing where the shaft turns by rolling on a set of balls. The rolling action gives very little friction. Puzzle from page 55: The method is to put the inner race inside the outer race, but pushed over to one side. The balls are then put into the gap where it is largest. Then the inner race is moved to the centre of the outer race and the balls moved round so they are evenly spaced. Finally the cage is put into position as two halves, one from each side, and joined together by rivets.

Bearing A part of a machine which allows a shaft or axle to turn easily.

Boiler The part of the locomotive where water is boiled to make the steam.

Connecting rod Connects the piston to the crank to turn the wheels. Has a 'big end' and 'little end'.

Crank Like a pedal on a bicycle. It converts a push-pull motion to a rotating motion.

Cylinder Round and smooth tube which contains the piston. The cylinders and pistons are the parts of the locomotive where the power in the steam is converted into the useful motion of the train.

Drain valves (Cylinder drains) Valves to let water escape from the cylinders when they are cold.

Drilling machine Machine for turning drills to make round holes in wood and metal.

Firebox The metal box which contains the fire. It is completely surrounded by water.

Gauge (of track) The distance between the two rails.

Lathe Machine tool for making parts which are mainly round - e.g. Wheels.

Milling machine Machine tool for making parts which are mainly flat - e.g. Connecting rods.

Piston Round disk which fits perfectly and slides in the cylinder. Steam pushes on the piston to turn the wheels by using the connecting rod and crank.

Piston ring A springy metal ring which helps the piston make a good seal in the cylinder.

Piston valve A type of valve for controlling the steam in the cylinder. (A slide valve is similar.)

Plain bearing (Journal bearing) Simple type of bearing where the shaft rotates in a metal sleeve.

Points (set of)	Junction between two tracks where trains can be switched from one to the other. Sometimes called Turnouts or, in America, Switches.
Pressure	When a lot of steam is squashed into a closed space, its pressure rises. Pressure is often measured in 'pounds per square inch' (or 'psi' for short).
	A pressure of 100 pounds per square inch means that on every square inch of the boiler shell or piston, the steam is pressing with a force of 100 pounds.
	A square inch is about 6 square centimetres or the area of a 10 pence coin.
	100 pounds is about 40 Kilograms or probably the weight of a young person.
	(The metric unit of pressure is the 'Newton per square Metre' or 'Pascal'.
	A Newton is a force equal to the weight of about one tenth of a kilogram.
	100,000 Pascals is called one 'Bar' and one Bar is equal to about 15 psi in old units.
	So 100 psi, the working pressure of Fiery Fox, is equal to a pressure of 6.5 Bar.)
Pressure gauge	Device in the locomotive cab which shows the steam pressure in the boiler.
Regulator	Main steam valve used by the driver to control how much steam is used in the cylinders. The more the regulator is opened, the harder and faster the locomotive works. (The regulator is often called the throttle in America.)
Rivet	A soft metal pin with a head at one end, used to join two bits of metal. The parts are drilled and the rivet dropped through. Then the straight end is bashed with a hammer to squash it into a second head to hold everything tight.
Sleepers	Cross beams which hold the metal rails to the correct gauge. ('Ties' in America.)
Steam	When water boils it bubbles and turns into steam. Normally steam has a huge volume compared to the water it came from. However in the boiler it is contained in a closed space and so instead of expanding to a large volume, it rises in pressure.
Tender	Large locomotives have a tender behind them to carry supplies of coal and water.
Turning loop	Loop of track for turning a train round. (Sometimes called a Balloon Loop.)
Turntable	Turns a locomotive round so that it faces the other way for a return journey.
Water gauge	Device in the locomotive cab which shows the water level in the boiler.

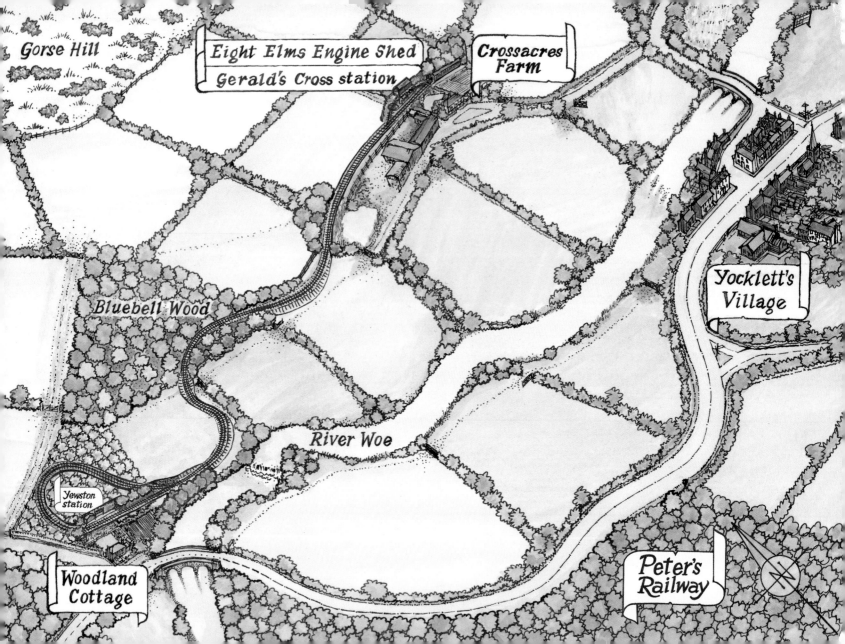

Gorse Hill

Eight Elms Engine Shed
Gerald's Cross station

Crossacres
Farm

Bluebell Wood

Yocklett's
Village

Yewston
station

River Woe

Woodland
Cottage

Peter's
Railway